PRACTICAL GUIDE TO IT PROBLEM MANAGEMENT

IT Pro Practice Notes

Practical Guide to IT Problem Management
By Andrew Dixon
2022

PRACTICAL GUIDE TO IT PROBLEM MANAGEMENT

Andrew Dixon

CRC Press
Taylor & Francis Group
Boca Raton London New York

CRC Press is an imprint of the
Taylor & Francis Group, an **informa** business
AN AUERBACH BOOK

First Edition published 2022
by CRC Press
6000 Broken Sound Parkway NW, Suite 300, Boca Raton, FL 33487-2742

and by CRC Press
4 Park Square, Milton Park, Abingdon, Oxon, OX14 4RN

© 2022 Taylor & Francis Group, LLC

CRC Press is an imprint of Taylor & Francis Group, LLC

ISBN: 978-1-032-21729-1 (hbk)
ISBN: 978-0-367-63622-7 (pbk)
ISBN: 978-1-003-11997-5 (ebk)

DOI: 10.1201/9781003119975

Typeset in Berling
by SPi Technologies India Pvt Ltd (Straive)

CONTENTS

Contents

BIOGRAPHY

Andrew Dixon currently heads the Service Management Office within IT Services at the University of Oxford. During his career, he has been both consumer and service provider before specialising in IT Service Management and ITIL for the last ten years. After completing his degree at University of Bristol, his first post was teaching Information Technology to engineering students. He went on to manage the computer teaching facilities for the Engineering Faculty at University of Bristol, providing a full range of services across a range of platforms. He has been responsible for data centres, networks, servers, desktops, printers, corporate applications, databases, websites and a host of other systems and services. He is both an ITIL 4 Managing Professional and an ITIL v3 Expert. He has presented at a variety of national and international conferences on a wide variety of topics, but his main focus now is on how ITIL may be used to transform and improve services.

INTRODUCTION

> Now, here, you see, it takes all the running you can do, to keep in the same place. If you want to get somewhere else, you must run at least twice as fast as that!
>
> – The Red Queen, *Through the Looking Glass*, Lewis Carroll

Some IT organisations seem to expend all of their energy fire fighting – dealing with *incidents* as they arise and fixing, or patching over, the breakage. You may have experienced or even work for an organisation like this. In organisations like this, restarting computers is seen as a standard method to resolve many issues. Perhaps the best way to identify whether an organisation understands *problem management* or not is to ask what they do *after* they have restarted the computer. If restarting the computer fixes the issue, it is very tempting to say that the incident is over and the job is done. Problem management recognises that things will not get better if we take such an attitude and that organisations will spend their time running to stay in the same place.

This book is a combination of methodologies including understanding *timelines* and *failure modes*, *drill down*, *5 whys*, *divide and conquer*; together with an exploration of *complexity theory* and how automation can assist in the desire to *shift left* both the complexity of the problem and who can resolve it. It is important to understand that establishing the *root cause* of a problem is not the end of the process as the resolution options need to be evaluated and then prioritised alongside other improvements. We will also explore the role of *problem boards* and *checklists* and the relationship between problem management and *Lean* thinking. As you progress through the book, it will provide you with both a framework for tackling problems and also a toolbox from which you can select the right methodology having identified the type of problem being faced. As well as reactive methods, it will present proactive activities designed to reduce the incidence of problems or to reduce their *impact* and complexity should they arise.

Solving problems is often a combination of common sense and methodologies which may either be learnt the hard way or which may be

DOI: 10.1201/9781003119975-1

taught. It is hoped that this practical guide will encourage you to adopt the tools presented within it, understand how and just importantly when to apply them, and in so doing upskill your staff and improve your processes.

ACKNOWLEDGEMENTS

I would like to thank Hannah for her encouragement to write this book and for providing the introduction with the publisher, Mark for his comments and advice on the draft version and John for his guidance.

CHAPTER 1
GETTING YOUR PRIORITIES RIGHT

This book is not designed to help you pass an exam in *problem management*, although it may help you set up a problem management process within your organisation (Chapter 10 looks at formal processes). Above and beyond that, this book looks at the bigger picture of how problem management adds value to an organisation and why it is important.

Take, for example, the *Apollo 13* moon mission. This is an oft-quoted example because of the famous expression

Okay, Houston, we've had a problem here.[1]

We could, at this point, concern ourselves with the nature of a *problem*. Rather, I want to initially focus on what was important at that moment as the three astronauts and Mission Control tried to understand what was happening. They needed to know the impact of what had happened. They did not need to know what had happened, or why it had happened. For some time, they did not need to know what they would do about it – that came later. The first question in problem management (and indeed in the related discipline of Major Incident Management) is:

WHAT IS THE IMPACT?

Let us consider the event from the view of the astronauts (Table 1.1):

In Chapter 5 we will explore how to ask the right questions at this point. The *impact* was assessed as:

Oxygen is required for power, heating and breathing. Oxygen has and is being lost. Without sufficient oxygen, the astronauts will die.

DOI: 10.1201/9781003119975-2

Table 1.1 Status in the initial minutes[2]

Incident:	'pretty large bang'
Readings:	Main B Bus undervolt
	Oxygen tank 2 was empty and tank 1's pressure slowly falling
	The computer on the spacecraft had reset
	The high-gain antenna was not working
Observations:	'a gas of some sort' venting into space
	The volume surrounding the spacecraft was filled with myriad small bits of debris from the accident

Normally, in such a situation, they would have used the Service Module's main engine to return to Earth, but they determined that there was a significant *risk* that it had been damaged in the explosion.

WORKAROUNDS

In problem management a solution which addresses the immediate impact issues without addressing the underlying *causes* is known as a *workaround*. In the case of *Apollo 13*, they realised that they had a spare source of oxygen – the Lunar Module and a spare source of propulsion – the gravity of the moon. The astronauts lived in the Lunar Module for the next four days whilst the spacecraft travelled to the moon and back, using the Lunar Module's propulsion system to guide the whole craft. This preserved the resources in the Command Module, so that it could be used for re-entry. The astronauts survived and were hailed as heroes, as were the staff of Mission Control who had assessed the impact and provided the workaround.

ITIL 4 defines an *incident* to be

> An unplanned interruption to a *service* or reduction in the quality of service.[3]

The explosion and subsequent readings and observations amounted to a serious incident.

ITIL 4 defines a *problem* to be

> A cause, or potential cause, of one or more incidents.[4]

The incident was over once the mission was over and the astronauts were safe. The tank which had exploded was somewhere in space – so it couldn't be repaired.

The problem remained. Before another *Apollo* mission could take place, they needed to understand what had happened and how they could remove or reduce the risk of it happening again. This is called *root cause analysis*.

Note that although evidence was gathered, it was not important that this analysis was done until after the workaround had brought the astronauts home. In any problem, mitigating the impact is the first priority. Sometimes, this can only be done by identifying the root cause and addressing it. However, that is not always the case and is a call to make.

The review board determined that Oxygen Tank 2 was faulty before the mission and that activating a fan within the tank caused an electric arc which caused the fire and explosion.[5] There were a number of contributing factors. The tank was later redesigned to remove the risk from all of the contributing factors. Performing the review was critical to the success of later *Apollo* missions – any one of which could have ended in disaster if the root cause analysis had not been done correctly.

The root cause analysis identified both a sequence of events which led to the accident and a design fault:

1. Tank 2 was originally in *Apollo 10*, but was removed to fix a fault. It was dropped when it was removed.
2. There were thermostats which were designed to operate at 28 volts, but were powered with 65 volts – they failed to operate correctly.
3. The temperature gauge was only rated up to 29° Celsius (84° Fahrenheit), so failed to detect the failed thermostats.
4. During testing, tank 2 needed to be emptied and the drain system didn't work, so they boiled off the oxygen. Without the functioning thermostats, temperatures may have reached 540° Celsius (1004° Fahrenheit).
5. The high temperatures appear to have damaged the Teflon insulation.

Tests on similarly configured tanks produced telemetry readings which were in accord with the telemetry readings captured during *Apollo 13*'s flight, which gave the investigators confidence that this is what had happened.

PREVENTING PROBLEMS

Problem management does not occur in a vacuum. When I trained to do First Aid at Work, one of the things I was taught was that it was better to avoid an accident than to pick up the pieces afterwards. If I saw a trip hazard, I could remove it or wait until someone tripped and then administer first aid. If I saw a drawing pin on the floor, then I could pick it up and put it back on the noticeboard, or I could treat someone with a drawing pin in the foot.

The cost of the *Apollo* series of missions is estimated at $25.4 billion, so it can be argued that this mission cost in excess of $1 billion and failed to achieve its primary objective of reaching the moon. The mistakes which led up to this were, therefore, very expensive mistakes.

The thermostatic switches used in Oxygen Tank 2 should have been replaced when the operating specifications were changed.

When the tank was dropped, it should have been fully tested in an end to end lifecycle test.

Oxygen Tank 2 was filled during a countdown demonstration test. When it could not be emptied using the correct procedure, a workaround was applied of boiling off the oxygen (which would normally be stored in liquid form).

At each point, if a different decision had been taken then this disaster may not have happened and a $1 billion mission may not have failed.

Problem management exists in the context of providing an end to end service and needs to operate alongside enterprise architecture, continual improvement and risk management.

Workarounds should not be used to pass the problem further down the line. If the drain pipe did not work, this should have indicated that there was a more serious issue in existence. Just removing the oxygen ignored the issue.

A NO BLAME CULTURE

There is no suggestion in this case that people covered up a story, but it is good practice in problem management and in its sister major incident management to operate a no blame culture. People make mistakes. This is part of human nature. We all make mistakes. If someone is doing their job and makes a mistake, there should be no blame attributed to them. Clearly, if they wilfully avoid safety rules or if they persistently fail to follow process, then that is a different situation. However, it is not helpful to blame someone for a genuine mistake. The first reason why it is not helpful is that people will conceal information if they believe that they will get the blame – valuable time will be lost trying to gather data which people could provide but which will incriminate themselves. The second reason is that tomorrow we all have to work together. I once accidentally deleted an entire web site. I had double-checked that I was only deleting a backup copy of it, but still managed to delete the live site. If I had pretended that it wasn't me, it would have taken ages to conduct fault diagnosis in order to understand what had happened. Because I immediately owned up to it, we recovered 90% of the site in under an hour and the complete site by the close of the day.

The *Apollo 13* mission is a useful case study because it was a complex *problem* with a number of *causes* which could have been avoided. Once the *incident* had occurred, the immediate need was for a *workaround*, which was successfully applied. Afterwards a full analysis identified the *root causes*, which could then be addressed. Above all, it is an example of a team which worked well together under pressure and were clear as to what their priorities were.

SUMMARY

Problems are the causes of incidents. If the impact of the incident is sufficient to warrant it, the problem needs to be investigated.

Rule 1: Assess the impact first.

Rule 2: Provide a workaround when appropriate. Sometimes it is more important to address the incident rather than the underlying cause.

Rule 3: Understanding the root cause allows reoccurrences of problems to be avoided.

Notes

1   https://en.wikipedia.org/wiki/Apollo_13
2   https://en.wikipedia.org/wiki/Apollo_13
3   ITIL Foundation: ITIL 4 Edition, Axelos Ltd, Stationery Office, 2019
    https://www.axelos.com/store/book/itil-foundation-itil-4-edition
4   ITIL Foundation: ITIL 4 Edition, Axelos Ltd, Stationery Office, 2019
    https://www.axelos.com/store/book/itil-foundation-itil-4-edition
5   https://en.wikipedia.org/wiki/Apollo_13

CHAPTER 2
TIMELINES

Let us assume that you have identified a *problem*, but you do not know what is causing the problem. A good place to start is by collecting a history or sequence of *events* and creating a *timeline*.

When you go to see a doctor because you are ill, they will typically do three things: they will ask you for your *symptoms* (what you think is wrong with you, what you can feel), they will look for *signs* (by taking your temperature and your blood pressure and by prodding and poking you), and they will take a history. In taking a history, they want to collect two sets of data. They want to know when the pain started and how it has developed. Is the pain the same at all times of the day or does it vary according to your activities? It may ease overnight and then return during the day. It may be worse when you are lying down and improve when you are upright. Collecting the history of the pain and other symptoms is important but there is another set of data which the doctor will also typically ask about. They also want to know whether your routine has changed. Have you been out of the country? Did you just run a marathon? A change in your routine may have caused or contributed to the illness. I am highly unlikely to have contracted malaria if I have stayed in the UK all my life, but if the doctor is told that I have just returned from a country where mosquitoes are prevalent, then they will pay more attention to that possible cause of my ailment.

In *problem management*, the collecting of a history and the creation of a timeline are also interested in those two sets of data. Is the *problem* continuous or does it vary according to the time of day or according to the *patterns of business activity* (see below)? Just as importantly, what is the context in which this is happening? Problem management is closely aligned to *change enablement* and arguably you will struggle to do problem management well if you do not implement change enablement.

Timelines

One of the most important questions that problem management asks is, 'what has changed?'

A change to the *system* may have been made automatically or may have been made by a user or an operator of the system. Automatic changes to systems include such changes as Windows updates. Even a restart to a system counts as a change to a system. Note that a Windows update may have been made earlier in the week, but not been applied until the system is shutdown or restarted. There is evidence that many end user *incidents* occur first thing on a Monday morning. Why do they happen then? There are many possible reasons, but the fact that many PCs are left on during the week and then switched off on a Friday means that updates only take effect during the Monday morning start up. Hardware failures also often occur at power up. Understanding what has happened, the history or sequence of events helps you to know what to look at.

User-led changes also cause incidents, but rarely cause significant problems. However, they should not be ruled out. If a printer has been extremely reliable for a long period and then becomes highly unreliable, constantly causing printer mis-feeds, it is worth asking the users if there has been any change to the way they are using the printer. It may be that there is a new user who is unfamiliar with how to load paper into the printer and is loading the paper the wrong way up. These days most paper is bi-directional, but in the early days of photocopiers the paper had a special coating on the topside and the paper wrappers had an arrow on the end to indicate the orientation. Loading paper upside down tended to increase the prevalence of mis-feeds.

Operator- and administrator-led errors do occur during changes. This is why change enablement is so important. How changes are recorded is less important than that they are recorded.

Once a history for the problem has been created, with a timeline, the changes which have been made to the system may be compared with the timeline to see whether there is any correlation. Sometimes it is easier to work backwards if there is reason to believe that a change is the cause of a problem. Either way, you should be looking for both positive evidence and negative evidence. An example of positive evidence is that a change occurs and then problem-related incidents start happening. Suppose that a Windows update is rolled out and each time a user applies the update to their PC, it then suffers the problem. This would suggest that the problem is related to the Windows update. An example of negative evidence is where problem-related incidents occur prior to the change. If some users have not applied the Windows update, but are still experiencing the problem, then this provides evidence that the update is coincidental and that the problem probably resides elsewhere. Note that it is very easy to miss the nuances associated with this. Windows updates often require a restart of the system. If there is evidence that people suffer the problem after a Windows update, but the Windows update itself has been ruled out, then you need to consider the system restart as a factor. Did the users who did not apply the update but did suffer the problem also restart their PCs? One problem which I have encountered was the result of a configuration change on a server. The configuration change was made one month earlier, but the server was not restarted, so the change did not take effect. The next month, the server was restarted after receiving its Windows update. The *service* running on the server failed. Everything pointed to the Windows update being at fault. However, once it had been rolled back and ruled out, a comprehensive history was taken and the faulty change identified.

PATTERNS OF BUSINESS ACTIVITY

Mapping patterns of business activity is a way of describing the busy and quiet periods of a service or of an organisation. Some businesses are very busy at the end of each month or at the end of a quarter, whilst universities are typically more busy during teaching term time and less busy during the students' vacations. Equally, many businesses will be busier during normal office hours and less busy overnight. Certain batch processing tasks will occur overnight because the systems are under less load at that time.

There are a variety of reasons why it is important to understand the patterns of business activity when considering a problem, not least to understand the *impact* of that problem. If there are performance issues as staff start work, then there may be two reasons for this. The obvious one is that everyone is starting to use the system at the same time. A second reason to consider is whether the overnight batch processing tasks have completed on time or are over-running.

Some problems only occur during busy periods of the year. If you consider the Tax Office web application for people to submit their tax returns (in the UK this is operated by HMRC–Her Majesty's Revenue and Customs), then although people can submit their tax returns at any point in the year, the web site becomes busier and busier as the deadline date approaches (the self-assessment deadline for online submissions is the 31st January each year for everyone). It is essential that IT staff understand the patterns of business activity for their organisation in order to anticipate surges in *demand* such as this. In the next chapter, we look at failure modes and the inability to cope with demand needs to be considered alongside other failure modes.

CASE STUDY: DATABASE CORRUPTION

During this book, I am going to recount some genuine problems which I have encountered during my career, without naming and shaming the individuals or their companies. Some details may be altered for the sake of illustration and dramatic effect.

A particular company had two major corporate applications which shared data and which required a nightly export of shared data changes from one application for import into the other. A problem developed in the export and the data was being exported in the wrong format. This had happened in the past and the team worked on it for a month with little success and with increasing concern about the deviation between the two systems. The *service owner* came to me for advice when it became apparent that they did not have the requisite skillset to resolve this situation.

Like a doctor in a doctor's surgery, I first arranged a consultation. I met with the service owner and with members of their team to understand the symptoms and collect signs. I also took an initial history of the problem.

I then went away and accessed their *ITSM tool* and looked at the incidents related to the problem to create a timeline of how these incidents related to the problem. It became apparent that there were two problems which were related in terms of symptoms, but not in terms of root cause. Early in the month there had been a change which had caused incidents. The change had been identified and corrected and the incidents had stopped. A while later the incidents had started again. It was clear that although the team believed that it was the same error, actually the symptoms were different and the signs were different. I refined my broad-brush timeline and concentrated on a more narrow time window based on when the second set of incidents had started. By the end of my analysis, I was fairly confident that something had happened on a particular day, even though it was not clear what that event was. I turned to the change enablement records in their ITSM tool. They had a good system for recording changes to the service and to the servers which it ran on. However, the implementation dates were sometimes vague. A Windows update was recorded as having been applied sometime during the week. A configuration change had been made sometime between two dates within the month. I identified five changes which might have been made on that date. None of them appeared to be a smoking gun. None of them seemed likely candidates for the errors being seen.

I arranged a second consultation with the technical members of the team and explained my thinking. I explained why I thought that this was the most likely date for a change. I listed the changes from their ITSM tool which could have been made, expressing doubt that any were likely candidates. The team considered each change in turn and ruled them out. They then referred to their team log and noted that an engineer from the vendor had been granted access to the system on that date.

I asked what the engineer had been doing. The engineer was not meant to be making changes in that part of the system, but it became apparent that they had. The company went back to the vendor with a complaint and a demand that they fix the issue. The issue was fixed in due course.

In my report I emphasised that a change enablement system is only as good as the data in it. It is really important that vendors follow the same process as the company. Vendor changes must be pre-approved and they must be recorded within the change enablement process. When a vendor is making a change, it is a good idea to ask for a *method statement* explaining what they are going to do and how they are going to do it.

SUMMARY

Rule 1: Create a timeline for the problem. Start with a broad-brush timeline and then fill in details where it adds value.

Rule 2: Cross-reference your timeline with changes from your ITSM tool and with system logs and other sources of information.

Rule 3: Look for negative evidence as well as positive evidence. Look further back in time to ensure that you are not missing evidence.

Rule 4: Try to distinguish between different problems which may have similar symptoms but different root causes.

Rule 5: All changes to a system should be recorded, including changes made by the vendor.

CHAPTER 3
FAILURE MODES

Failure modes are descriptions of the various ways in which a *system* can fail. Suppose you have a Windows PC on your desk and you get a blue screen of death – when the PC stops working and displays an error message on a blue background. You will restart the PC and carry on. This is a single *incident* and it is normally not worth worrying about. Suppose you keep getting a blue screen of death. You clearly have a *problem* and you will want to address that problem so that your work is not constantly interrupted. So, the first question to ask is, what different components of your Windows PC could cause a blue screen of death? Understanding what components could fail is the study of failure modes.

There are two reasons why it is valuable to understand failure modes. The first is to know where to look when a system fails. The second is to determine whether the reliability of a system could be improved by reducing the likelihood of certain failures.

We can break a Windows PC down into at least three layers – the hardware, the operating system and the applications which run on the operating system. Any of those three layers could cause a blue screen of death. One possible cause is a memory fault. Memory faults could happen at any of the three layers. Running the Windows Memory Diagnostic Tool might reveal which layer is at fault. Equally, it may be a case of following the *timeline* and establishing what behaviour causes the crash. It may occur only when a particular application is run. It may occur only when a certain amount of memory has been used.

For people working on a *Service Desk*, it is useful to list the different failure modes for a Windows PC. At first glance there only appear to be a few failure modes – I listed only three above. In practice, there are multiple failure modes within each layer. Each of these can be further broken down. The following list may be helpful:

POSSIBLE FAILURE MODES FOR A DESKTOP WINDOWS PC

1. Loss of electrical power
   a. area wide power cut
   b. RCD trip at the fuseboard
   c. fuse in the plug has blown
   d. the power cable is loose or poorly connected
   e. the PC switched mode power supply may have failed
2. Hardware failure
   a. memory failure
   b. hard disk failure
   c. video card failure
   d. fault on motherboard
3. Loss of network connection
   a. fault with local area network (LAN) or network switch
   b. loss of connection between LAN and Internet
   c. loss of connection between PC and network switch
   d. network card failure
   e. network software fault (e.g. *DHCP* or *DNS*)
4. Operating System conflict
   a. Software bug in latest Windows update
   b. Windows update interrupted and became corrupted
   c. Device drivers conflict
5. Application
   a. Software bug in application
   b. Application designed for an earlier or later version of operating system
   c. Conflict between application and device drivers or other applications

This is not an exhaustive list but is indicative of the multiple layers where a failure could occur. If an end user contacts a Service Desk to say that they cannot connect to their favourite web site, then the Service Desk analyst has to consider all layers and all failure modes and work in a logical way to identify where the fault lies.

The failure modes for a simple server are not dissimilar, but we typically add complexity to server infrastructure in order to add *resilience*. I define resilience as the ability for a system to continue to provide its main service despite the failure of an individual component. If the hard disk of my Windows PC fails, then I have lost the use of my Windows PC until it is repaired and I may have lost all data which was written to that hard disk since my last backup. Whilst this may be acceptable and tolerable for a single desktop computer, it is not desirable for a corporate server. To improve resilience, servers typically have RAID disks (Redundant Array of Inexpensive Disks), dual network connections and dual power supplies. RAID disks protect against the failure of a single disk within the system by splitting the data across multiple disks with a layer of redundancy in the data (so that one or more disks may be removed from the array without losing any data). Dual network connections protect against the loss of the network interface or the loss of a single network switch. Dual power supplies which are plugged into separate power supply paths protect against the loss of the power supply unit, but may also protect against the loss of raw mains or of the fuseboard. Many commercial data centres certify 100% mains power supply, but only on the condition that each system is plugged into both the 'A' feed and the 'B' feed. They are permitted to remove either feed without notifying the customer.

The first important point is that if you wish to achieve a resilient system, then you need to map all of your failure modes and ensure that they are all resilient. Suppose dual power supplies are both plugged into the same power feed. This protects against the failure of the switched mode power supply unit, but not against power loss. Suppose dual power supply–fed servers are plugged into network switches which were fed from a single power supply. The servers would have stayed up during a power interruption, but could have been disconnected from the network.

A second important point is that it is essential to monitor for component failure. Failure to do so and respond swiftly delays but does not prevent incidents. For a large RAID array, there needs to be a replacement timeline agreed, so that failed disks are replaced and the RAID array rebuilt before the next disk fails. Suppose network routers are linked by two fibres following different paths. If one fibre fails without anyone realising, then if the other fibre is damaged the link would be broken.

When a *complicated problem* arises (see next chapter for a discussion of different types of problem), the standard method of problem resolution is to seek the *root cause* and then either fix the root cause or find a *workaround* to mitigate or minimise the problem. In order to find the root cause, it is important to understand the different failure modes, so that they can be eliminated in turn and the root cause identified.

CASE STUDY: A VIRUS OUTBREAK

Computer viruses and malware are an ever-present threat. Once they breach a corporate boundary, they can spread extremely quickly. A review conducted after a zero-day virus outbreak identified that the security system had failed to prevent the spread of the virus at a number of layers. If the virus had been contained at any one of these layers, then the spread would not have occurred or would have had considerably less *impact*. The failure modes which were identified were as follows:

1. A malicious email breached the mail firewall boundary
2. The malicious email was not picked up by the mail virus checker
3. The user opened the malicious email even though it was suspicious
4. The user opened the attachment of the malicious email
5. The malware Trojan horse was able to run on the local PC (the anti-virus software did not detect it because it was a new variant)
6. The malware Trojan horse was able to download a payload from the internet through the firewall
7. The payload virus was able to run on the local PC (the anti-virus software did not detect the virus either)
8. The payload virus was able to write to local disk, network disk and to the user profile

It is worth noting that resilience is about multiple layers of defence – in this case they all failed. Placing infected PCs and infected profiles into quarantine was effective in stopping the further spread of this zero-day virus, but due to a high rate of re-infection, it was only when the failures could be addressed (with virus signatures provided by the anti-virus companies) that the problem was resolved. The clean-up operation was hampered because initially the infected computers were quarantined but the failure modes were not adequately understood. When the user, whose user profile had been infected, moved to another computer, their profile was downloaded from the server and infected the second computer. Collecting timelines and infection statistics quickly showed this up and the user profiles were also quarantined. During the review process, each of the failure modes was considered and, where possible, addressed.

SUMMARY

Understanding how computers fail, their failure modes, assists in the root cause analysis of problems.

Rule 1: A resilient service is only as resilient as the weakest link

Rule 2: It is best practice to improve security at multiple levels so that if one level fails, you do not lose all security. This is known as Defence in Depth

CHAPTER 4
COMPLEXITY THEORY

The *Cynefin Framework*[1] defines problems into four categories:
- Obvious
- Complicated
- Complex
- Chaotic

We will look at these in turn.

OBVIOUS

Many *incidents* are never classified as *problems* since it is obvious how to fix them, they are unlikely to re-occur and there is no benefit in doing problem management on them. An obvious example of this is a paper jam in a printer or photocopier due to the paper being fed in incorrectly. How to remove the jammed paper is usually obvious and the user then needs to insert the remaining paper correctly. If this is an infrequent occurrence, then it does not need problem management. If it occurs frequently, then there may be a training issue. Just occasionally the obvious problem turns out not to be obvious and standard problem-solving techniques are required.

Complexity Theory says that for *obvious problems*, the resolver should **sense** the issue, **categorise** it according to previous experience and **respond** accordingly.

COMPLICATED

A problem is defined to be *complicated* if it has a single *root cause* for which the resolution is not obvious. The root cause may not be known, so it is not always possible to state up front that a problem should be classified as complicated. The standard method of resolving complicated problems is to do *root cause analysis*. Later chapters of this book will look at a number of techniques for conducting root cause analysis in order to resolve complicated problems.

Case Study – Reprographics Printer

Most paper jams are counted as obvious problems. They are often the result of untrained staff adding paper incorrectly. As explained in Chapter 2, many people do not know that printer paper has an upside and a downside and it used to be the case that certain printers were more susceptible to jamming if the paper was inserted the wrong way up. With many printers being capable of dual-sided printing these days, this problem has largely disappeared. Whilst the careless feeding of paper into the trays may still be an issue, this case study concerns a reprographics unit using a very high-spec, high-speed copying unit where this was not the case. All staff were highly trained. They rarely had paper jams until on one occasion they neared a particularly busy period of the year and the unit started repeatedly jamming. Initially they treated the problem as obvious and cleared the jam and carried on. The frequency of paper jams increased and some observations were taken. A *timeline* was recorded in order to understand the behaviour of the problem. The jams didn't occur when the unit was operating at normal load. They occurred only when a particularly long run, or several medium runs back to back were in progress. They concluded that the unit had a fault which was manifesting itself during high usage. The first thing they did was to apply a *workaround*, which was to break long jobs up into several medium jobs and to spread these jobs out across the day, interspersed with smaller jobs. This worked, but was extremely inconvenient and increasingly impractical as they reached the busiest point in their year. They did, however, have enough evidence to contact an engineer from the photocopier company and complain that the unit was not achieving its published throughput ratings. The engineer came and examined the unit in great detail and could not find a fault. Then the engineer looked at the paper that they were using and asked when the company had changed paper suppliers. During a quiet period of the year, the company had indeed changed paper suppliers to one offering a slightly lower grade at a cheaper price. This paper was rated for use by normal photocopiers, but the engineer explained that it was inappropriate for the high-speed unit in reprographics which ran at a much higher temperature than normal photocopiers do, especially during long runs. The paper was degrading during these long runs, and this was causing the paper jams. The engineer had identified the *root cause* and recommended that the company purchase a higher grade of paper for this particular unit.

Complicated problems have a *single* root cause. Sometimes a workaround can be identified prior to the identification of the precise root cause. In the case of the above example, some initial observations (the timeline) identified when the paper jams were occurring but not the precise reason why. This allowed the team to apply a workaround which enabled them to continue to operate whilst the problem was investigated. Further analysis will usually reveal a root cause with a certain level of certainty. It is not always possible to know beyond doubt that a particular cause was the root cause, but the problem is considered resolved if the problem disappears when the probable cause is addressed.

Complexity Theory says that for *complicated problems*, the resolver should sense what is happening, **analyse** the available data (including an accurate timeline) and then **respond** accordingly.

COMPLEX

As was mentioned in the previous chapter, computer systems are becoming ever more complex. It is increasingly the case that some problems do not have a single root cause. It may be that a number of components have all partially deteriorated or failed. It may be the case that no individual component has failed at all, but that the interaction between components is no longer within tolerance. Problems where there is no single root cause are called *complex problems*.

Whilst there are standard techniques for discovering the root cause of a *complicated problem*, it is more difficult to deal with a complex problem. Priority should be given to ameliorating the situation by use of *workarounds*. It is sometimes possible to identify partial root causes. Where possible, these should be addressed. There is no guarantee that these will cause an immediate improvement. This yields two frustrations. The obvious one is confidence. In a complicated problem, if there are grounds for believing that the degradation of a particular component is the root cause, then fixing that component should fix the problem. If it does, this adds evidence and confidence. In a complex problem, fixing that component may not improve the situation significantly if at all. Without this improvement, it is difficult to know whether the change which has been made should remain in place or not. A general rule of thumb in *problem management* is not to change too much and not to change more than one thing at a time. This rule works extremely well for complicated problems. It can hinder complex investigations. The second frustration occurs if fixing a partial root cause results in a worst service than before. In a maze it is sometimes necessary to walk in the opposite direction in order to move forwards. The same is true with complex problems, but it is very difficult to justify certain levels of trial and error if it is necessary to carry this out on the production system itself – it is much easier if the problem can be replicated on a *development system* and the trial and error takes place there. Unfortunately, complex problems often manifest themselves differently on development and production systems. This should not be seen as only a negative outcome. Sometimes, the different behaviour on different systems may be utilised as part of the *divide and conquer* technique (Chapter 7) in order to narrow down the possible causes of a problem.

An example of the increasing complexity of some problems was a recent issue with a corporate application generating an error at login for some users but not others. The usual problem diagnostic methods were deployed and no one could identify any changes which might account for the behaviour, nor any differences between those who could access the application and those who could not. The vendor's knowledge base was consulted again and a new post identified similar behaviour being reported by other customers. Following this up, it was discovered that the corporate home page, running on an entirely separate platform, was setting a new cookie which was being consumed by the corporate application due to cookie inheritance. This new cookie contained JSON code which the corporate application could not cope with.

Employees who visited the corporate home page before attempting to login to the corporate application were being denied access, whereas those who used different browsers for the two sites were unaffected. How this was diagnosed is less important to this example than the fact that two applications which did not share any data or platform interacted in a way which had not been anticipated. Increasingly, no application exists within an island. How we diagnose problems needs to recognise this. There were two root causes. One was a bug in the corporate application, and the other was a change to the cookies on the corporate web site. Once the behaviour was understood, a simple workaround was communicated to users, to either clear their cookie cache or use separate browsers or an incognito window. This provided time to plan changes to fix both causes.

Complexity Theory says that for *complex problems* the resolver should **probe** the system and then **sense** how it responds to the probing before **responding** accordingly.

CHAOTIC

It is sometimes the case that any change to a system seems to make it worse. In this case, the problem is described as *chaotic*. The Cynefin Framework recommends that where a chaotic problem arises the objective is to make changes which will transform it into a *complex problem*, which may then be addressed. We should also consider why chaotic problems occur. It may be the case that a chaotic problem is the cause of poor management or deliberate, malicious action.

A standard method of recovery from a chaotic problem is to wipe the system and rebuild. This is particularly important if the chaos has been caused maliciously. Consider a virus infestation. If an individual PC has been infected, then it is theoretically possible to examine the system and clean it. However, if the behaviour of the virus is poorly understood and the infestation has not been caught quickly, the quickest route is to wipe the hard drive and reinstall from a known good backup (or from scratch). It is important to consider network drives within this. Some viruses will infect files on network drives. If the local system is rebuilt, but the network drives are left intact, then as soon as the user logs back in they can re-infect the PC. Macro-enabled documents and spreadsheets or applications which are shared across network drives, should be checked before users are allowed to continue to use them.

In an Agile or DevOps situation, poor *change enablement* could result in multiple changes to the different levels of a system being made at the same time. A network change, a database change, an application change and a web interface change could all occur at the same time and cause a chaotic system. Reverting to a known good situation is the best approach in situations like this.

It is worth remembering that a *timeline* is still worth establishing even when a chaotic problem is believed to exist. If a system has to be rebuilt from scratch, it is important to know to which point in time it should be built and therefore which versions of each software item.

Complexity Theory says that for a *chaotic problem* the resolver should **act** first and then **sense** before **responding**.

SUMMARY

Understanding the nature of the problem will assist with which techniques are used and how they are used.

Note

1   https://en.wikipedia.org/wiki/Cynefin_framework

CHAPTER 5
AUTOMATION AND ARTIFICIAL INTELLIGENCE

There are a number of products on the market which proclaim problem solving capabilities using *artificial intelligence* techniques. In this chapter, I will explore the capabilities and attractions of these products in a generalised way, recognising that their capabilities are constantly evolving.

It should be noted that these products are typically aimed at *obvious* and *complicated problems* and not at tackling *complex* and *chaotic problems*. The use of artificial intelligence in problem solving may be broken down into identification, diagnosis and resolution.

IDENTIFICATION

Automated tools are good at two activities which lend them to problem solving. The first is large-scale processing of data, and the second is pattern matching. Keeping a diverse fleet of end user devices patched and updated to the latest software and device drivers is a complicated and time-consuming task. At their simplest, automated tools can offer to automatically identify software which does not have the latest patches and, if directed, to apply those patches to the software. Note that there is a complication here in that some updates are free and should always be applied and others have licencing implications. An automated tool cannot apply those updates without authorisation.

Given that patches are typically released to address bugs in software which could otherwise lead to *problems*, this is a form of proactive *problem management*.

Products with built-in artificial intelligence may go further than this and monitor systems for undesirable behaviour such as 'Blue Screen of Death' (BSOD) *events* or a series of errors in the event log. If a computer suffers multiple BSOD events, then it is likely that there is an underlying issue and the automation tool should flag this to the local support team.

Pattern matching may be performed for an individual PC (such as multiple BSOD events), but it may also be performed across the whole fleet of computers. If the events logs of multiple computers are all recording the same error at a particular time each day, then this may be picked up by an automated tool far quicker than by human operators, who will not see the pattern unless it results in multiple incidents. It has been observed that users of computers have become so used to computer failures that they rarely report minor issues because they have so little confidence in them being resolved. However, intelligent systems may be able to identify trends and address them.

DIAGNOSIS

It is not clear that current automated tools are conducting intelligent diagnostics for themselves. They may flag an event for further investigation by the local support team, but the tool does not need to understand the cause of a BSOD event to know that there is an underlying problem.

If the automated tool does provide a higher level of diagnosis, then it may appear to the organisation using it to be highly intelligent, but this higher level of diagnosis may in fact be the activity of engineers working for the third party who provide and support the automated tool. In addition to keeping the patching list up to date, engineers may also diagnose problems which their system has identified. Edging into the area of artificial intelligence, the automated tool may conduct pattern matching on all the errors which it has detected within a given period of time (e.g. all the BSOD on a given day) and look for common attributes which connect these systems and which are more prevalent within this population than in the wider computer population. Engineers can then look at this information in order to try to discern a *root cause*. As a theoretical example, it may be that the pattern recognition software identifies that BSOD events are more likely to occur if an older version of an office productivity suite is used in combination with an up-to-date version of a marketing tool application. The pattern recognition software may also identify that the systems concerned also have social media management applications in common; however, if this marketing tool application utilises the office productivity suite to send emails, then a causal link may be established between those two applications whereas the other applications may have no relationship to each other. The engineers could then check compatibility notes (which an artificial intelligence tool would not typically be able to do) in order to establish whether the functional requirements for the marketing tool application mention specific versions of the office productivity suite. If this is a known error, the engineers can configure the automation tool to flag up the inconsistencies to the local support teams. Note that it is not a problem which can be fixed by the automation tool in isolation since there are licensing implications to address. Upgrading the office productivity suite to the latest version is not free and would require new software licences.

RESOLUTION

An automation tool can be involved in resolution at different levels. If a software patch is identified during the diagnostics stage, then the automation tool can deploy that patch without a support person needing to visit the end user device. Whereas identification of a hardware fault would involve the local support team. Within the context of a data centre, the automation tool may identify that a server is at risk of failing and remove the server from the production cluster, moving services onto other servers. The data centre team can then repair the server in their own time.

SHIFT LEFT

There are a number of ways in which automated tools offer a shift left capability to organisations.

At their simplest, they provide an identification service which ensures that more issues are picked up earlier and that missing patches are applied in a more timely way. IT departments are shown in a positive light if they proactively contact users and address their issues before the *Service Desk* is contacted for support.

Proactive *problem management* also reduces the scale of problems. If a hard disk is identified as about to fail before it actually fails, then the disruption to the end user or the server cluster may be reduced.

There is also a theoretical idea that *complex problems* occur because *complicated problems* were missed and were allowed to develop into complex problems. This will not always be the case. However, there are examples of *chaotic problems* with multiple root causes where some of those root causes could have been identified earlier and the problem may never have developed into a chaotic problem.

SUMMARY

The use of automated tools provides a level of proactive problem management which should not be dismissed, even though it may appear to only address minor issues. Automated tools are very dependent on the support infrastructure which surrounds them. If they are not kept up-to-date, then their value will deteriorate extremely quickly.

CHAPTER 6
DRILL DOWN

There are *obvious problems* where the root cause has been seen before and is well understood, but for which it is important to be able to quickly identify which of a range of *root causes* is presenting on any given occasion. This is particularly important for *Service Desk* analysts who will be presented with a particular scenario and need to work methodically through that scenario to identify which root cause has resulted in the behaviour being exhibited. Service Desks have a number of aims, of which one is to resolve, on first contact, as many *incidents* as possible (the first contact fix rate). They also wish to minimise the number of incidents which result in a second line engineer needing to visit on site to resolve the incident. If the Service Desk analyst (SDA) can identify and resolve an incident during the first contact (whether that is a phone call, a chat session or a walk in), then this is an efficient use of resources. One common way to achieve this is the use of the *Drill Down* technique, and this is commonly applied with the aid of conditional *checklists*. We will explore the use of checklists in more detail in Chapter 14, but the conditional checklist is a technique whereby the SDA will ask a series of questions from a checklist and the answer to one question will determine the next question asked. In theory, at the end of the checklist the SDA will know which root cause has exhibited this behaviour and therefore what cause of action should be followed. In some cases, this will be an escalation to a second or third line team; in others it will necessitate a remote session to the client PC in order to apply a fix. Drill Down is the technique which is employed to facilitate this. Drill Down can be used without conditional checklists but is particularly efficient when used with their aid.

The objective of Drill Down is to take an exhibiting condition which could have multiple causes and drill down into the issue to understand what is causing it. Collecting additional information allows scenarios to be ruled out and determines what further questions need to be asked in order to drill down further. The Drill Down technique is not restricted to the *obvious problem* domain but works particularly well where most root causes have been encountered before. This is because the SDA will know what questions to ask.

One of the strengths of Drill Down is that it does not assume a solution in advance, but works methodically to rule out solutions in order to drill down to the correct solution. It is frequently used in industries where the product range is very limited and the range of common faults is well documented and classified, such as Internet Service Providers (ISPs). It should be noted that some users will have a high technical understanding and the indiscriminate use of Drill Down alongside conditional checklists can frustrate such users. This is not, of itself, an argument for not using them, but SDAs should use them intelligently and listen to the user in order to discern under what circumstances they can be circumvented. It may be worth asking a few *stratified questions* at the start of every conditional checklist in order to avoid unnecessary effort. The most common one of those would be 'Have you seen this before?' There is no guarantee that the issue is the same as before, but the Drill Down could be shortened in order to ascertain whether this is a repeat occurrence or not.

HYPOTHETICAL CASE STUDY

This example is given to demonstrate how the technique might work in a Service Desk scenario. Imagine that a user phones the Service Desk early one morning to say that their Outlook email client will not work. Without Drill Down, it would be tempting to spend some time looking at Outlook options. However, the Drill Down technique says that a specific order should be adopted in diagnosing this type of scenario.

Question 1: 'Do we know whether the *service* is up and running?' For email, this should be straight forward, since the SDA can check whether their own instance of the service is working. For other services, the use of the corporate Service *Status Page* should identify whether there is a known error with the service. If there is no reason to believe, at this stage, that the service is unavailable, the Drill Down approach then takes a different tack.

Question 2: 'Is everything else working?' This may seem like a strange second question, but it is an important one. Users frequently present an issue which is only tenuously linked to the actual *root cause*. This question allows the SDA to understand whether the issue is actually related to the particular service (and its client) or is a broader issue.

There is an apocryphal story of the user who rang up an IT Service Desk to say that their desktop computer had suddenly stopped working. The Service Desk analyst asked for the Asset Tag and was told that the user could not read it. When asked why, they were told that there was a power cut and the lights had gone off. Clearly the computer was a victim of the power cut and the user needed to address that issue first.

Part of the purpose of Drill Down is to rule out other causes (such as a power cut) before assuming that the *presenting issue* is accurate and focussed.

Let us assume that the answer to question 2 is that google.com and bbc.co.uk both seem to be unavailable as well. This leads the SDA to believe that it is actually a network issue and not directly related to email. If the network was working as expected, a different line of questioning would be followed at this point.

Question 3: 'Is it just you or are other users affected?' Many users will work in an open plan office or in proximity to other users. If one user is experiencing networking issues it is important at this stage to assess whether this is a localised issue relating to just their PC, or whether it is a more general issue. Statistically, when a widespread IT outage occurs only a small number of users will report it immediately. Many will work around it by doing other jobs which are not impacted in the hope that it will fix itself. By definition, the first person to report a networking issue is reporting a new issue. It is helpful if the SDA can identify early on whether this is a widespread issue and this will be the first of many calls, or whether this individual has a particular issue only affecting themselves.

Although the root cause may differ dependent on the answer to question 3, the following questions will often be useful either way.

Question 4: 'Does the wired PC have lights illuminated alongside the
network socket?' Recognising that the SDA will need to talk
most users through how to identify this, it is very useful to know
whether there is a physical connection between the network
switch and the PC and having illuminated lights is a good
indicator of that. Not all network cards have lights (especially on
laptops) and the user may be connecting via Wi-Fi.

   If there are no lights, then the network switch may be down
(affecting a large number of users) or there may be an issue
with wiring. If this is the case, it is worth asking if anything has
changed. Do not rule out the possibility that the user has just
moved office and plugged their PC into a network socket in the
wall which looks identical to the one in their previous office, but
is not patched or is patched differently. You may think that users
would report that sort of information up front, but many do not
(especially if they moved last thing Friday and only switched the
computer on first thing Monday). The other thing to note is that
if they do volunteer this information, it is a good case for shorten-
ing the Drill Down sequence and jumping straight to question 4.

Question 5: Depending on the operating system, there will be a
standard diagnostics command which can be run to report on
network connectivity (e.g. `ipconfig/all` within a `cmd.exe`
window for Windows 10). This should identify whether the PC
is correctly connected to the network and has picked up all the
correct settings.

The above Drill Down is likely to reveal that one of four causes is to
blame (remembering the earlier discussion about *failure modes*). Either
there is a physical network fault, or there is a fault with the network
switch, or with *DHCP* or with *DNS*. One example might be that they
have indeed moved office, but the network appears at first to work –
with illuminated lights. However, because their PC was allocated to a
different subnet previously, the local DHCP server does not recognise
their PC and has not provided it with a valid IP address. This would be
identified by question 5. Eliciting why the DHCP server did not recognise the PC would be the next line of questioning. If the PC has moved,
then this is clearly the root cause. If it has not, then a restart of the
PC would fix the fault for a number of scenarios (without identifying
exactly which one). It may be that the DHCP server has been restarted

since the PC obtained its IP address and that the DHCP server has allocated the same address to another PC causing a conflict. In situations such as this the computer may have popped up an alert informing the user. However, users do not always understand these alerts and may have ignored it, not realising that it was related.

Note that the diagnostics command will typically indicate what state the network is in as far as the computer is concerned, but may not indicate why.

Once the SDA has completed the Drill Down, they should have collected sufficient information either to effect a remote fix or to triage the incident to the correct team to address.

It is worth remembering that this incident started with the user reporting an email issue, but after Drill Down it has been established that it was in fact a network issue totally unrelated to the email service. It is quite common for the presenting issue to not be related to the root cause. This is one of the reasons why the Drill Down technique is so useful.

SUMMARY

Drill Down works very well in situations where the resolver is trying to narrow down an issue which is likely to be a well-known issue, but which cannot be immediately identified for whatever reason (for example because the resolver is remote and is relying on the user to explain their issue).

Rule 1: Use a standardised checklist (see Chapter 14 for more information about checklists) to ensure a common approach.

Rule 2: Be prepared to short cut the checklist if there is good evidence for a probable cause or for eliminating certain options – don't treat users as idiots.

Rule 3: Each question asked should have a purpose and should enable the possible causes to be narrowed down further.

Rule 4: Remember that the presenting issue may be unrelated to the root cause.

Rule 5: Drill Down does not always find the cause. If a first time fix is not going to be possible, collect the appropriate amount of information and pass the incident to the correct team.

CHAPTER 7
DIVIDE AND CONQUER

In the previous chapter, we looked at *Drill Down* as a technique for diagnosing which component of a live system is causing a problem. Drill Down is a largely non-invasive technique which makes it ideal for *Service Desk* staff to use. A related, but subtly different, technique is often called *Divide and Conquer*. This is usually an invasive technique and involves isolating or changing components in order to identify which one is at fault. In Chapter 3 we looked at *failure modes* and this technique identifies the failure modes for a *system* and then isolates them. There will be different ways to do this depending on the design of the system.

Let's start with a simple example to explain the process. Suppose in an office there are two desktop computers, each with a single computer screen. One computer is working and the other is not. It would appear that power is not reaching one computer. Divide and Conquer identifies three top level failure modes – the mains socket may be dead, the computer lead may be faulty (such as a blown fuse) or the computer may have a fault. To start with, we will isolate these three different failure modes to identify which one is at fault. We can do this by switching off and unplugging the working computer and plugging the dead computer into the same socket. If it remains dead, then we know that it is not the socket at fault. Next we can swap power leads. This removes the possibility that it is a blown fuse. If either of these two stages results in a working computer, then we know that it is not the computer at fault and we can investigate in a different direction, but if it remains dead then we have confidence that it is the computer and not the environment which is at fault. The above can be carried out by the user, at which point they can call in a repair engineer with confidence. The repair engineer now considers the failure modes within the desktop computer. The two obvious ones are the switched mode power supply and the motherboard. If both of these are working, then one would expect some visual or audible clue that the computer is not totally dead. The repair engineer will isolate these two components by unplugging the power connection to the motherboard and testing it with a multi-meter. This should give a clear indication as to whether the switched mode power supply is working or not. If it isn't, then the repair engineer can replace it. There is a possibility that the evidence will point towards the motherboard being faulty, when in fact it is a component connected to the motherboard. Typically, before replacing the motherboard, everything else will be disconnected or unplugged to confirm that it is the motherboard itself.

My next example is domestic rather than computer-related. A kitchen has many appliances and in this scenario, the homeowner is regularly suffering power cuts. Typically twice per week the fuse board RCD[1] protection will trip for the kitchen circuit suggesting that there is a fault. However, it has been impossible to identify a single appliance which is causing this. How can we diagnose this fault? Divide and Conquer is an ideal diagnostics tool for a task like this (although PAT[2] testing would be advised as well). Suppose the homeowner leaves half their appliances plugged in and only plugs the other appliances in when they are actually using them. They keep a diary of which appliances are plugged in when the RCD trips. Each time the RCD trips they change the combination of appliances left plugged in (obviously always leaving the fridge and freezer on, but changing combinations of other appliances). It is almost certainly the case that the RCD trips are being caused by poor insulation within two or more appliances, each not sufficient in its own right to cause the trip, but together sufficient. With the use of the diary, it should be possible to identify two appliances which together cause the trip. It may be that there are three appliances contributing, but nevertheless the task is to identify two which are contributing first and then see if they together are sufficient. If the two on their own are not sufficient then a third needs to be identified. Once the appliances have been identified they need to either be repaired or replaced.

Software defects can also be identified using Divide and Conquer. Software developers may put break points in their code in order to examine the state of memory at a given point in order to establish whether a fault is occurring before or after that point.

CASE STUDY: CORRUPTED SURNAMES

A large organisation issued identity cards in an automated process which took a download from the Human Resources (HR) system each night, identified new employees and imported those new employees into the identity card system for production of cards the following day. However, one day the system stopped supplying the details of new employees. Initially the identity card team assumed that there had been a lull in appointments. After enquiries were made, they established that new employees were being entered into the HR system, but their data was not arriving in the identity card system. The IT department was contacted to investigate. The first action which was taken was to isolate the different systems involved in the process in order to identify where the fault lay. The process was quite complex with four computer systems and multiple tasks being carried out. In essence the four computer systems were the HR system, a middleware automation system which extracted the data from the HR system and created a table in a database on an interface staging system, and then this data was then passed to the identity card system. With three hops between the four systems, it was important to isolate them in order to identify which hops were still working and which were not. For a given day, the new entries were manually identified in the HR system and cross referenced with the entries in the interface staging system. It was confirmed that the data was successfully arriving in this database. A nightly script was run on this database. Log files showed that this script was generating an error and 'failing safe' by not sending data on to the identity card system since it had identified the data as corrupt. Unfortunately, the script as written didn't provide any valuable diagnostics data – either it succeeded, or it determined that the database was corrupt and failed to send any data. The script needed to be re-written to write to the log file details of which entry it had failed on. Once the relevant record had been identified, it was possible to examine closely how the script was treating that entry and why it was failing. The surname in question exceeded the character length which had been coded into the script and the surname was running into the next field in the record, resulting in the corruption being observed. Increasing the script to cope with longer fields fixed the issue. The identity card system field lengths were also checked, and it was confirmed that they matched those in the HR system; it was only the intermediary system which could not cope with the exceptionally long surname.

SUMMARY

Complex systems may be isolated into separate components using a process of Divide and Conquer in order to assess which component is suffering the problem. Understanding the failure modes within the system is very valuable in determining how to divide the components.

Rule 1: Identify possible failure modes

Rule 2: Design a test which will distinguish between one set of failure modes and another, thereby reducing the possible number of failure modes

Rule 3: Repeat this until it is possible to identify a single failure mode as a contributing factor

Notes

1   Residual Current Device
2   Portable Appliance Testing is an electrical appliance safety test process

CHAPTER 8
CAUSE AND EFFECT

A favourite anecdote of mine is of a computer manager who was frustrated that one of his servers kept crashing at the same time early each morning. He did all the usual diagnostic operations, including increased logging, to no avail. There was no apparent reason and no indication immediately before the server would crash that it was about to do so. Confusingly, the server would crash at more or less the same time each morning and then recover and restart itself automatically ten minutes later. Eventually, the manager decided that he needed to sit at the console and watch the server, so he got up quite early and went to his server room and sat watching the screen. Just before the appointed time, the cleaner walked into the server room and said 'hello'. She unplugged the server from the wall socket and plugged in her vacuum cleaner. When she had finished vacuuming, she dutifully plugged the server back in and it restarted.

Not all *problems* have technical *root causes*. Understanding the range of possible causes is important both for obvious problems and for more complex failures.

Major failures are often the result of multiple failures at the same time (as seen in the *Apollo* disaster). The analysis of this is attributed to Kaoru Ishikawa, who in the 1960s identified a number of factors which contribute to a problem or failure. His fishbone diagram reminds us that problems and failures are not just technical and therefore the prevention of recurrences is not just technical.

In understanding a problem, we need to consider:

- Strategy
- Environment
- Communication
- People

- Processes
- Equipment

If we look again at the five factors which together caused the *Apollo* disaster, then we can see how they may be classified according to the above:

1. Tank 2 was originally in *Apollo 10*, but was removed to fix a fault. It was dropped when it was removed.
2. There were thermostats which were designed to operate at 28 volts, but were powered with 65 volts – they failed to operate correctly.
3. The temperature gauge was only rated up to 29° Celsius, so failed to detect the failed thermostats.
4. During testing, Tank 2 needed to be emptied and the drain system didn't work, so they boiled off the oxygen. Without the functioning thermostats, temperatures may have reached 540° Celsius.
5. The high temperatures appear to have damaged the Teflon insulation.

We may see that there is a failing of *strategy* at multiple levels here. The re-use of equipment without a thorough understanding of the implications of that re-use lies at the heart of this disaster, contributing to factors 1, 2, 3 and 4 to a greater or lesser extent.

It may be argued that it is a failing of *strategy* when staff ignore mistakes (such as dropping the tank) and apply undocumented workarounds when things go wrong (such as boiling off the oxygen).

There were failings of *environment* with the use of equipment rated at 28 volts being used in a 65-volt environment and also of not being clear what the temperature range for equipment was (factors 2 and 3).

There was a clear lack of *communication* between teams in order to arrive at these factors, even though that poor communication may not have been spotlighted in the official report. Not all staff who work in IT enjoy writing documentation, but so many problems arise because when a change needs to be made no one understands the original specification. If we want to reduce the number of problems and increase the speed of resolution of problems, then we need to tackle poor communication and documentation.

The culture in which *people* work is a huge driver for the rate of problems within an organisation. Whilst I strongly believe in a no blame culture where we do not blame an individual for doing their job (unless they have been clearly negligent or wilfully disobedient), it is important to understand that the incidence of problems will reduce only if the culture which allows them to occur is tackled. In an industry such as space travel the culture must be safety first, but the *Apollo 13* disaster emphasised that NASA did not operate such a culture. Unfortunately, later disasters would suggest they did not learn this lesson.

Processes are put in place for a reason. It may be argued with hind-sight that factor 4 failed to follow process, although it was signed off at the time. This raises the interesting question of when alternative options should be considered and when they should not be. Finding a workaround for a failed process at the time of the failure can be fraught with danger. It is very easy to choose a process which appears on the surface to work but has unexpected consequences. Applying quick fix workarounds should always be seen as a *risk*-based activity where the risks of not doing it need to be balanced with the risks of doing it and it going wrong. In both this disaster (which wasn't fatal) and the space shuttle *Challenger* disaster (which was), the risk of launch delay was balanced with the risk of a catastrophic loss of the mission. It was later said of the *Challenger* disaster, 'Violating a couple of mission rules was the primary cause of the Challenger accident.'[1]

The *equipment* failed – that was the presenting fault, but it only failed because of other failures which had already occurred, and which had been ignored.

We may combine all these contributing factors together in a fishbone diagram (Figure 8.1).

In Chapter 3 we looked at *failure modes* and concentrated mainly on the technical/equipment failure modes. It is important to remember that there are wider issues to consider and not all failure modes are associated with the equipment itself.

CASE STUDY: DATA CENTRE FAILURE

When the air conditioning control system in a major corporate data centre failed, it took many days to restore all services. A review of the failure identified that it was not just an equipment failure which had

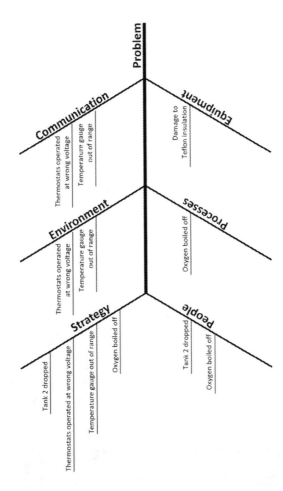

Figure 8.1 An example fishbone diagram.

brought the corporate applications to a grinding halt, but failings at many levels:

- The air conditioning control system failed (*environmental*)
- Automatic failover to another data centre failed (*equipment*)
- Manual *fail over* did not work first time (*process*)
- The same people were trying to recover multiple services (*people*)
- These people were not clear on the priorities for recovering services (*communications*)
- Not all disaster recovery plans were up-to-date and usable (*strategy*)

The loss of air conditioning was a known failure mode which should not have caused such widespread disruption, but the disaster was far worse than it should have been because this one failure was compounded by multiple other failures which could have been avoided.

SUMMARY

When considering failure modes and when tackling issues, do not only consider the technical, equipment-based vulnerabilities, but also consider other factors.

Rule 1: Consider all factors

Rule 2: If undiagnosed failures have already occurred, then problems may be compounded. Identify and fix them before they affect services.

Note

1 https://en.wikipedia.org/wiki/Space_Shuttle_Challenger_disaster#cite_note-18

CHAPTER 9
RESOLUTION EVALUATION METHODS

In Chapter 4 we looked at *complexity theory* and noted that not all problems have a single *root cause*. It is tempting to think that if a root cause (or multiple root causes) can be identified, then that is the end goal, the cause(s) can be fixed and normal operations resumed. *Problem management* in the real world does not end with the identification of the root cause.

ALTERNATIVE SOLUTIONS

There are some *problems* which are caused by something which breaks or something which changes and breaks something. In cases like this, it is usually possible to identify the obvious fix. As the complexity of problems increases, even understanding the root cause of the problem does not guarantee a single solution. There may be different ways of fixing the problem (or applying a *workaround*). Where different options could exist, these need to be identified and a *risk* analysis undertaken for each one. The objective for each option is to determine both the likelihood that it will resolve the problem and any potential problems or negative consequences, in order to minimise the risk. Some options may fix the presenting problem but cause secondary problems or move the problem from one part of the *system* to another. Remember that in the *Apollo* disaster, the oxygen was boiled off to fix one problem, but caused a greater one.

A plumbing analogy for this is that if a pipe is blocked, applying water at high pressure carries two risks – one is that the increased pressure might break a joint or alternatively you might just move the blockage from one part of the system to another, maybe more inaccessible, part. It is tempting to think that if a disk fills up, moving the data to another disk will resolve the problem, but care needs to be taken that the second disk has the storage capacity required (not just at that moment but for a period of time), and that it also has the throughput capacity to cope with the additional demands being placed on it. One methodology available for this type of analysis is called Kepner-Tregoe.[1]

PRIORITISATION OF FIXING THE ROOT CAUSE

Once the optimum fix has been identified, the appropriate prioritisation of the fix needs to happen. It is sometimes the case that fixing a root cause is within the capability and normal operating budget of the operational team. If this is the case, then the root cause is likely to be fixed within a reasonable period. However, what is a reasonable period? Problem management does not exist in isolation and a single problem is rarely the most important issue confronting an organisation. Once a root cause has been established (or is deemed likely) an evaluation needs to take place to determine where the resolution of the problem lies in relation to other operational priorities.

CONTINUAL IMPROVEMENT

Some root cause resolutions may be achievable within the normal *Business As Usual* (BAU) operations of the organisation. If this is the case, then the proposed resolution should be added to the *Continual Improvement* register and prioritised alongside all the other service improvements being considered. The cost benefit of resolving this problem needs to be quantified in such a way that it can be compared with other priorities within the improvements list. As an example of the issues which may be encountered – suppose a problem is causing an hour's additional work to the operations team once a month, but is otherwise not adversely affecting the *service*. Clearly it would be beneficial to resolve this problem. It is not clear, however, that this should be done to the exclusion of all else. There may be two other competing claims on the time of the operations team. One may be a more obscure problem which only manifests itself every few months but is service affecting, whilst the other may be an efficiency suggestion rather than a problem. The implementation of the efficiency suggestion may save 2 hours per month. At this point, the cost benefit of each option needs to be evaluated together with the team capacity required for implementation. If the implementation of the efficiency suggestion is as cheap as, if not cheaper than, fixing the initial problem, it may be deemed better value for money since the net saving is 1 hour a month. Conversely, fixing the problem may only takes 3 hours whilst the implementation of the efficiency suggestion might take 30 hours to implement. If this is the case, the payback period may be deemed too long or the operations team may not have the resource to dedicate to such a piece of work. The service affecting problem will also have a cost benefit which may be more difficult to evaluate in the same way but it may be deemed a higher priority than either of the other two depending on the nature of the organisation and the predictability and *impact* of the outage.

Equally, it is sometimes acceptable to live with a workaround for a significant period of time rather than expend the energy involved in resolving the problem.

An example of this was a Java memory leak in an *ITSM tool*. The Java memory leak resulted in the application periodically crashing. Eventually two workarounds were applied. The first was to increase the amount of memory available to the application, which ensured that the application could run reliably for at least a week without crashing. The second was to restart the application once a week out of normal business hours. It is important to note that in this case a problem resolution was outside of the organisation's capability since it was a commercial product. It is not clear how quickly the supplier could have fixed the root cause, but the workarounds removed the immediate need for a resolution.

PROJECTS

Even when the resolution is within the control of the organisation itself, it is not always possible to implement a resolution within *BAU* operations. A new project may need to be established in order to fund and facilitate resources including staff time, additional software and hardware. For example, there may be a need for a major software rewrite or the hardware may require (directly or indirectly) an upgrade in order for the resolution to be made. In the case of commercial off the shelf (COTS) software provided by a third-party supplier, it may be the case that a major upgrade of the software is required in order to address this problem, but that major upgrade needs to pass through business change management as well as technical change enablement in order for the organisation to accept the upgrade.

If a project is required for implementation, then a business case will need to be made which sets out the direct requirement for the project (why it is important to fix the problem and why a project is required in order to do so) as well as any indirect benefits (such as additional features offered by the upgrade). The cost-benefits analysis will then need to be made using the same methodology as for any other project and the proposal fed into the project prioritisation process.

SUMMARY

Identifying the root cause of a problem does not mean that a fix should be applied immediately. An options analysis exercise should be conducted to consider all options and then a cost-benefits analysis exercise should consider this problem resolution in the context of the total work backlog of the team concerned. It is often the case that proposed fixes are added to a Continual Improvement register for consideration as part of a wider process.

Note

1   https://www.kepner-tregoe.com/

CHAPTER 10
ITIL PROBLEM MANAGEMENT

In their *ITIL 4* framework, Axelos Ltd define the practice of *problem management* as being distinct from the *incident management* practice. Reactive problem management involves responding to *incidents* which have already occurred in order to understand the underlying *causes* and address these. Proactive problem management is about identifying *risks* and responding to those risks before they manifest themselves in incidents.

PROACTIVE PROBLEM MANAGEMENT

A key component of proactive problem management is to have a well-defined patching policy. Security risks may be reduced by routinely deploying security patches issued by vendors in a timely manner. Many organisations understand the need for security patches, but fail to take seriously the need to deploy other patches. Patches and hotfixes are issued for two reasons. One is feature enhancements; the other is addressing defects in the design of the product. If defect patches are not deployed, then by definition there are unresolved *problems* within your product. Patching policies are needed not just for software applications but also for the firmware which comes with hardware. There was a recent case where a hardware vendor, HPE, identified a fault with the firmware within some of their hard drive products.[1] A particular model of SSD drive would fail with total loss of data after 32,768 hours (less than four years) unless the firmware was updated. This is an extreme case where the vendor was proactive in informing their customers of the need to upgrade the firmware. Hardware vendors produce firmware updates on a regular basis, and it is important that each organisation has a patching policy for how frequently they will respond to these updates.

One of the best ways of doing proactive problem management is to learn from other people's incidents. Following the industry news can be useful for alerting you to major, widespread issues. As an example, there are regular reports on the effects of Microsoft's Patch Tuesdays (the date each month when new Windows updates are issued) on the stability of the computers receiving the patches. However, being part of a support community can add greater value than this. Sharing your experiences and then learning from other people's experiences is useful in its own right, but also provides greater leverage with vendors. Vendors are more likely to address an underlying issue if multiple clients are pursuing them, but if those clients are working together this may add extra weight to their individual voices. I have known vendors who claimed that teething issues with a new software application were local to our organisation, but when I spoke to other organisations using the same product it was apparent that the issues were ubiquitous. We were able to apply greater pressure on the vendor when we combined to speak with a common voice.

Various techniques mentioned earlier in this book, such as *failure mode* analysis, are important tools in proactive problem management. There is value in conducting an independent audit of an end to end *service* in order to assess the risks to that service.

PROBLEM CONTROL

ITIL 4 recommends that a key aspect of problem management is the process developed for controlling and managing problems. Each problem which is identified (either through reactive or proactive problem management) should be recorded in a problem record within an *ITSM tool* or similar system. Problem records should be linked to related resources. In reactive problem management, the related incidents should be linked to the problem record. *Configuration Items* (CIs) such as desktops, servers, printers and software assets should also be linked to the problem record as required. The problem record is a way to:

- collate the information
- prioritise the effort
- coordinate who is involved

- spin off tasks for people to engage in to progress the problem diagnostics and resolution
- keep a historical record which may be referred to should a similar problem occur in the future

Each problem record will have a lifecycle. Note that different stages in the lifecycle may overlap. Some organisations prefer greater granularity in the lifecycle, whilst others will utilise a more coarse approach, but the following stages may be helpful:

- *Logged*: a problem record is created because a problem is suspected. At this stage, the problem has not been confirmed. In reactive problem management, a logged problem record indicates that there is a suspicion that a group of incidents may be related and that the problem has not been seen before. In proactive problem management, it may be that an issue has been identified in another organisation but it is not clear at this stage whether that issue will affect your organisation.
- *Identification*: this is a confirmation stage where a consistent problem is confirmed and ideally is reproducible. Data is collated at this stage. A trawl through recent incidents may surface further ones, which were not initially identified, as being related. A prioritisation process needs to happen at this point to determine how much effort will be devoted to this problem record. This is typically scored according to both *impact* and *urgency*. Some problem records will be left at this stage because either the impact or the urgency is low. They will be reviewed periodically to see whether new data (e.g. additional incidents) warrant a change to the priority.
- *Investigation*: The problem solving techniques outlined in this book may be employed in order to identify one or more *root causes* or other possible means of progressing the problem.
- *Known Error*: ITIL defines a *Known Error* to be a problem which has been analysed but not resolved. From a problem resolution point of view, this is not an important stage. However, it is useful for the *Service Desk* to have a list of current Known Errors, together with an explanation on how to identify whether an incident is related to them and also what action should be taken if one is encountered. It is worth reflecting on the frustration experienced by Service Desk analysts if they spend

time trying to resolve an issue for a customer, fail, refer it to second line and are only then told that this is a known error.

- *Workaround available*: The role of incident management is to get users/customers back up and working as quickly as possible. It is often possible to identify a *workaround* which will achieve this as an interim solution whilst the permanent solution is sought. In an earlier example, I noted that clearing the web browser cookie cache before visiting a web application provided a viable workaround (as did accessing it from an incognito window). Whilst this was not a desirable action to have to take for any prolonged period of time, it did allow users to carry on working whilst the IT teams identified the right solution and implemented it. Where there are outstanding incidents, the workaround needs to be communicated to those users. Some workarounds become permanent workarounds. It should be noted that these increase the organisation's *technical debt* and need to be added to a *Continual Improvement* register.

- *Root Cause Identified*: Whilst not all problem records get to this point, it is hoped that for significant problems (problems with a high impact or a high urgency), the root cause will be identified within a reasonable timeframe.

- *Evaluation*: It is tempting to jump straight from identifying the root cause to fixing it. It is important to include an evaluation step first. Chapter 9 looks at resolution evaluation methods to discern the best way of addressing a root cause. It should be remembered that not all root causes should be fixed. In some cases, a workaround may be deemed to be adequate. In the case of the cookie clash previously mentioned, two root causes were identified. An evaluation needed to be made to determine whether one or both would be fixed. The evaluation decided that the cookie needed to be fixed because it might impact other web-based applications as well, either now (but not yet identified) or in the future. The corporate application was also patched, because a patch was available and recommended by the vendor. Whether this was essential or not was subject to a *risk* assessment. It was decided that it was easier to apply the patch than to run with the risk of this happening again. It should be noted that applying the software patch took a number of days of staff effort and if the impact of this problem had been less, this might not have been considered cost effective.

- *Resolving the root cause*: Having evaluated the optimum means of fixing the root cause, this needs to be added to the work queue for the relevant teams, appropriately prioritised alongside their other work. Adequate testing of any changes to the system need to be done before the fix is implemented and normal *change enablement* processes followed. Once the fix is in place, the result on users who have been affected needs to be evaluated. Sometimes the fix at the server end will not resolve the issue for the end users, who may also need to make a change on their desktops (e.g. clearing the cache). If users are still using a workaround, they need to be notified that the permanent fix is now in place. The Known Error may be removed from the Service Desk list of current problems once this has been completed.

- *Long-term monitoring*: Unlike incidents which should be marked as resolved as soon after resolution as possible, a problem record will typically be left in a semi-open state for a period of time in order to assess whether the fix which has been applied has been effective. Not all fixes address all issues. If the incidents reoccur, then the problem record should be re-activated and moved back to the identification stage. However, it should be noted that it is often the case that the incidents for two related problems will all be linked to the first problem record. If there is evidence that the first problem has been successfully fixed, but that a second problem exists with a different root cause, then a new problem record should be created and the relevant incidents moved across. As a general rule of thumb, an incident should not be linked to two problem records as there should not be two independent problems causing it (as distinct from one problem with multiple root causes).

- *Closed*: a problem record which has been monitored for a reasonable length of time, with no recurrences may be marked as closed.

KNOWLEDGE MANAGEMENT

One key aspect of both proactive problem management and reactive problem management is knowing how data is meant to flow between systems. It is common practice in large organisations for integration platforms to be used as midpoints between different corporate applications. Data is not shared on a point to point basis, but is shared to the integration platform, which then passes the data on. Whilst there are many technical and operational benefits to this approach, it can obscure how the data is used. Periodically changes are made to the meta data for corporate applications – in some cases this will be the addition of a new field, in some cases it will be the change in format of a field (e.g. extending the field length to allow for longer surnames or changing the encoding for a field from 8-bit ASCII to 16-bit UniCode). In other cases it will just be a change in the contents of the dataset such as agreeing that invoice codes can now be 6 digits rather than 5 digits or adding new country codes to reflect a changing political horizon. It is important to recognise the knock-on consequences of changes to the data in one corporate application on the other corporate applications which are downstream consumers of that data. If change enablement does not adequately consider the implications of these types of change, then problems can arise sometime later. Tracking these problems back to the change concerned can prove time-consuming if records are not kept with sufficient detail of how the data is used.

Knowledge Management may be used both for keeping track of shared data about the services and systems available and for providing the Service Desk analysts with checklists for drill down and other means of resolving incidents.

SUMMARY

A formal practice and process for problem management, such as the ITIL 4 practice, is a good way of methodically keeping track of problems.

Note

1   https://support.hpe.com/hpesc/public/docDisplay?docId=emr_na-a00092491en_us

CHAPTER 11
PROBLEM BOARDS AND PROBLEM RECORDS

MANAGING PROBLEM RECORDS

Within *ITSM tools*, there is usually an option to create *problem* records which can be linked to *incidents*. The *Service Desk* should link incidents to existing problem records where the behaviour is consistent with them being related.

Many low-priority problems can be dealt with as *business as usual* by the teams who have the expertise to resolve those problems. As a general rule, I recommend that Service Desks do not create problem records and pass those records on to technical teams, but that each team is responsible for its own problem records, which it should communicate to the service desk so that they can link the incidents to them. If a team believes that another team should have a problem record which appears not to exist, then an alternative means of communication may be used to recommend the creation of a new problem record. If a problem record has been created by one team and it becomes apparent during the diagnosis that the issue lies within the jurisdiction of another team, then they should be contacted and invited to take ownership of the record. Owning a problem record does not imply that only one team can undertake tasks associated with the issue, but indicates which team is driving the investigation.

PROBLEM BOARDS OR SWARMS

There are times when a problem spans the expertise of multiple teams and having one team own the problem record is not sufficient to facilitate resolving it. Where significant or major problems exist, which need the expertise of multiple teams, it is best practice to form a *problem board*. Although these are typically constituted as formal meetings, they do not need to be and will operate in different ways in different organisations, but the general principle will remain the same. Problem boards are created for the express purpose of tacking one issue and their membership should reflect the issue being tackled. They bring together expertise from multiple technical teams, together with representation from the Service Desk and often have an independent coordinator. Sometimes, they will include representation from the business area which is being directly affected.

Whilst this book will talk about problem boards, an alternative approach of gathering a *swarm* should also be considered. Swarming is different in as much as it tends to be used in the Agile world to describe teams tackling a well-understood problem together in order to find the best solution.

ASSIGNING CLEAR ROLES

Where the resources and technical expertise of a single team are insufficient to resolve a problem, it is very important to assign clear roles within the problem resolution process. For significant problems, it may be appropriate to form a formal problem board to manage the problem in order to ensure that multiple teams are working together effectively.

Whether a formal board is formed or the problem is tackled in a more light-weight manner, being clear who is performing what role is very helpful:

- Coordinator
- Communications
- Technical lead
- Application lead

- Management liaison
- Note taker
- Service Desk representative

HOW PROBLEM BOARDS WORK

When a problem board is first formed, it will meet to agree its terms of reference and assign roles. It also needs to establish whether the appropriate resources are available. It will discuss the problem in hand and consider the following aspects:

- *Impact* – how serious is this problem and what is the impact of it on the business, how many users are affected?
- *Urgency* – how quickly does it need to be resolved?
- *Workarounds* – are there any workarounds for the users affected by this problem? Note that the availability of a workaround may affect the impact and urgency of the problem, but it is a good idea to assess the impact and urgency both with and without a workaround unless it has already been confirmed to address the immediate issue.
- The *timeline* of the problem – when did users first start noticing the problem? Is there any system information such as event logs which would indicate when the problem first occurred?
- Changes – the change records in the *ITSM tool* should be compared with the timeline to identify whether the problem has been caused by a planned change
- Plausible causes of the problem and any techniques which could be used to corroborate or eliminate specific causes should be discussed
- What further diagnostic information is required to investigate this further?
- Are the appropriate technical experts available and engaged? Note that as new information is obtained, the requirements may change, and additional technical experts may need to be brought on board.
- A list of SMART (Specific, Measurable, Achievable, Realistic, and Timebound) actions should be agreed and documented, which teams should then undertake to progress the investigation

Problem Boards and Problem Records

Problem boards typically meet on a regular basis to review progress and work through the process. It is important to record the meetings promptly, being clear what actions each team/individual is being asked to undertake and when they need to report back. The use of a business communication platform such as Microsoft Teams can be very valuable for holding documentation concerning a problem and also allowing the investigators to chat about any findings as they arrive, rather than hold information back until the next meeting (although traditional mailing lists may also be used).

Many of the case studies in this book have grown out of problem boards which I have attended.

THE 5 WHYS

The 5 *whys* is a technique which I find particularly useful in the context of problem boards. In essence it is the same as *drill down* (Chapter 6). In drill down an expert will ask the customer a series of questions in order to narrow the possible range of *causes*. In the 5 whys technique, a non-technical person (such as the chair of the problem board) will ask a technical expert a series of questions in order to home in on the root cause. When a technical expert is asked why an event has happened, they will typically give a fairly general statement as to which sub system of the service they believe to be at fault. Note that the 5 whys technique asks why this has happened rather than what has happened. If the storage has failed, it is usually fairly easy to state that the storage has gone off line. From the point of view of *root cause analysis*, the important question is why? An example might be as follows (noting that this may span multiple problem board meetings as more data is collected):

Chair: Why has the *service* failed?

Expert: The storage *system* became unavailable

Chair: Why did the service not *fail over* to the other site?

Expert: The virtual machines continued to run, but hung waiting for their storage

Chair: Why did the storage system become unavailable, when there are two controllers?

Expert: Both controllers ran out of memory at more or less the same time and the first was still restarting when the second failed

Chair: Why did both controllers run out of memory?

Expert: We are talking to the supplier about this, it looks like a bug in the controller firmware

Notice that although it is described as a 5 whys process, it is not essential to ask precisely 5 whys. The point is that the dialogue should continue until it is clear why the behaviour occurred in order to be able to ask the question of what should be done about it. In this case, there were two actions which could be taken: one to reduce the likelihood that the memory capacity would be exceeded, and the other was to request a firmware patch from the supplier.

WHAT HAPPENS WHEN PROBLEM MANAGEMENT DOESN'T WORK?

We learn not just from our successes but also from our failures, so I include an account of when a problem board didn't resolve an issue. During the Covid-19 pandemic many call centres which had been based in corporate buildings ended up in people's own homes. One such call centre had been operating in this new way very successfully for a year when it started having problems. The staff were using work-supplied computers to connect through the work VPN (virtual private network) onto the call centre system. Suddenly they started to find that if their broadband dropped the VPN connection, then when they re-connected the call centre client on their computer would not re-connect to the call centre system. This was not consistent; rather, it only happened intermittently, but it was becoming disruptive to the business, so a problem board was set up. At the first meeting, representatives of the various teams were brought together – the telephony team, the desktop support team and the networks team. An independent chair discussed the scenario and took the teams through the timeline. There were no changes logged around the time of the first occurrence and no clues other than the relationship between the failures and the VPN. The meeting agreed a set of actions in order to progress the problem. The VPN client being used was an in support and fully patched version, but was not the very latest version, so it was agreed that the telephony team would trial the newer version. Key staff being affected would be contacted and asked to collect more detailed information about the exact time the incidents occurred, which the networks team would then be able to use to track what was happening by comparing this with the events log for the VPN servers. The desktop support team would evaluate a diagnostics tool which could run on the users' computers and might collect more detailed routing information.

All of this is good problem management process. We never found out whether it would have got to the root cause, because before the second meeting of the problem board the issue was resolved via a different route. A separate incident came in from a project team concerning the call centre *development system* and when the networks team diagnosed that incident, they discovered that there was a routing mismatch and that some traffic destined for the production system was being re-directed to the development system in error. The routing table was adjusted and the problem disappeared. The timeline was double-checked. The routing change had been correctly logged some months previously. It was only when there was increased activity from the project team on the development system that the error impacted the production service.

The conclusion is that problem solving techniques are not perfect and sometimes they won't help. However, having a consistent methodology is far better than searching for a needle in a haystack, even if it is not always the quickest method. In my experience, if people can fix it quickly, they will do so without recourse to using these techniques. Problem management is valuable when that option has failed.

SUMMARY

Where a problem spans the expertise of multiple teams it may be advantageous to form a problem board to coordinate the effort and encourage effective collaboration.

CHAPTER 12
THE DRIVE FOR EFFICIENCY

THE RELATIONSHIP BETWEEN EFFICIENCY AND PROBLEM MANAGEMENT

Whilst it may not at first sight be apparent that efficiency is related to *problem management*, there are a number of reasons why efficiency may be regarded as a form of proactive problem management. When we think about the complexity of problems, then it is worth noting that the more streamlined and efficient a process is, the easier it should be to identify and therefore to resolve any issues which arise. Equally, in making a process more efficient it is often the case that very minor problems are eliminated at the same time. These minor problems may not have been significant enough to ever warrant problem management attention, but their elimination will benefit the organisation over time.

Reflecting on the cause and effect of problems and noting that not all problems are technical, there are a number of techniques available today which can assist in product optimisation and efficiency. Whilst optimisation and efficiency are not directly related to problem resolution, it should be noted that some problems arise because processing is too slow or bottlenecks have occurred. In cases like this, the use of *Lean* is appropriate.

USING LEAN TO OPTIMISE PROCESSES

The Lean methodology, which was derived from a production method used by Toyota from 1930, aims to remove waste and inefficiency. It looks at the whole value stream (the end-to-end process used to produce a product) and identifies eight types of waste.

Defects

Lean uses the term 'defects', but these may be thought of as *problems* affecting the output of a system. Anything which causes the product the user consumes to fail to conform to the standards and specifications required may be considered to be a defect. This may be the result of incorrect source data, software bugs which incorrectly process that data or hardware issues which corrupt the data.

Excess Processing

There is a maxim which states that data should be processed only once. Many people are aware of systems which should talk to each other but which are not integrated and the result is that operators have to manually re-type data in order to transfer it from one system to another. This is an extreme example of excess processing, but there are other examples where a poorly designed system expects the operator to make calculations which the system could do for them, or they have to remember information between different screens. There is a significant risk where data has to be re-typed that errors will be introduced. Even the number of clicks required to achieve a simple task may be classified as excess processing.

An example from the ITSM world was a university Service Desk which was required to log an incident for every person who came to their walk up desk. Many of the visits could be classified under one of ten headings and did not require further follow up (headings included purchasing consumables, resetting passwords, providing routine advice). Quick action links were provided which enabled the Service Desk analysts to record these events with the click of one button, rather than multiple clicks. The data was collected, but not at the expense of the Service Desk staff.

Overproduction

In a factory setting, it is obvious that producing too many products is unnecessary and creates both cash flow issues and storage issues. It may be less clear in an IT scenario what is meant by overproduction. Lean is not just interested in the end product, but in the overproduction of components. In IT teams, it may be helpful to think about the layers of a typical client server application. Typically, a client interface (often web-based) will talk to a web server, which will in turn talk to an application server, which will in turn talk to a database server. In order to scale up a service and provide resilience, there are usually multiple servers in each layer. Assuming that *demand* for this service fluctuates both according to time of day and according to the seasons, then there is no need to run the maximum number of servers all the time. Clearly, the service needs to be able to cope with peak demand when necessary, but it should be able to scale up and down to meet that demand. Some infrastructures will do this automatically, but other infrastructures require this to be a manual process. The typical consequence of it being a manual process is that the number of servers is rarely changed and there is 'overproduction' of servers for much of the time.

A potential problem is caused by this inflexibility if the anticipated peak demand is exceeded and performance drops as a result.

Waiting

The obverse of overproduction is waiting – where a user has to wait for a service because there is insufficient resource available at the time that they wish to use it.

This may on occasion be measured in fractions of a second, when they have to wait for a screen to update because the servers or other infrastructure have not been scaled to match demand. Another form of waiting is for maintenance. Older computer systems were often designed in such a way that maintenance and updates require the whole service to be taken off-line whilst the change is made. It may be possible to do this at a quiet period of the day, but it is sometimes the case that a few users still have to wait for the service to be restored.

Increasingly, we are seeing systems designed in such a way that some servers can be taken off line and upgraded whilst the service continues to be provided on the remaining servers. Once the first group of servers have been updated, they are returned to the pool and other servers are taken off line in order to be upgraded. This means that the service need never be unavailable and removes this form of waiting.

Inventory

Holding excess stock does not at first sight seem to be related to problem management. It is, however, a real problem for large IT organisations who purchase desktops, laptops, servers and storage arrays in large quantities. Economies of scale mean that they are encouraged to buy in bulk. However, this needs to be balanced with the demand and also with the ability to commission and deploy the equipment. In a badly organised company, it is possible for excess computer equipment to sit in store rooms beyond the warranty period or even in extreme situations beyond the supported lifetime. Universities in the UK suffer from a poor accounting technique which does not allow individual departments to carry over surplus revenue from year to year. As a result, it is quite common for IT departments who have an excess at the end of a year to advance purchase equipment for the next year. Sometimes, that equipment will sit in boxes for much of the year because staff do not have the time to commission it, or the project it was bought for was not ready to use it. The consequence of this is that the lifespan of the equipment is shortened or the equipment is made to run beyond its support contract increasing the risk of it failing outside of its warranty period.

Transportation

Processes which involve the frequent or routine movement of physical equipment need to be evaluated to consider whether the transportation of those goods is optimal. There are organisations where business units purchase their own IT equipment and have it delivered locally. The IT department then needs to collect that equipment and take it somewhere else to be commissioned before returning it to the right business unit. This is highly inefficient. Even the location of storerooms within a building should be considered to determine whether the processing route is optimal.

Motion

Another aspect of transportation is the number of visits to the data centres which are required for routine operations. Many data centres now operate on a 'lights out' basis where there is no need to visit the data centre to manage the equipment at all. Other data centres see daily trips to change backup tapes, commission new equipment on a piecemeal basis and a wide variety of other activities which could be managed in a more structured way. The cost of these daily visits should be compared with the cost of additional equipment which could negate the need.

Non-Utilised Talent

Computer systems lend themselves to automation and scripting, and yet highly technical teams often find themselves doing routine and repetitive tasks because it is easier to keep doing the repetitive tasks than to find the time to upskill the staff and develop better ways of working.

One of the consequences of manual repetitive tasks is that mistakes creep in and problems result. Checklists are a way of both reducing this type of error and enabling more junior members of a team to perform these tasks.

Identifying Value

One of the emphases of Lean is to identify where the value is derived within a process and within a value stream and increase that value whilst reducing the waste.

A side product of undertaking Lean is that when a *problem* does arise, the overall process should be better understood and it should be easier to identify the *root cause*.

CREATIVE PROBLEM SOLVING

The Lean methodology also provides a technique called Creative Problem Solving which in essence encapsulates the concepts contained within this book in a single cycle (Figure 12.1):

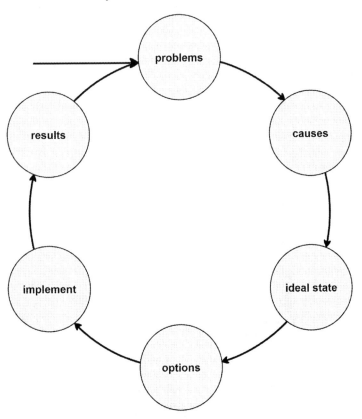

Figure 12.1 The creative problem solving cycle.

In the first stage of this technique, the problem is identified and goals agreed. *Root cause analysis* is then applied to the problem. *Resolution evaluation* methods are treated in two sections in this technique as the ideal state is first articulated and then options are evaluated against this ideal state. When the problem is a clear case of something not working, then an ideal state is usually obvious, but in the real world this is not always the case and it can be important to ensure that all members of the problem team are agreed on what 'good' looks like. Only once the options have been evaluated and a best option chosen can a solution be implemented. The results then need to be measured to ensure that the desired outcome has been achieved. If it hasn't, then the cycle may need to be repeated. If it has, then the next highest-priority problem may be tackled.

SIX SIGMA

The Six Sigma methodology also grew out of manufacturing and places emphasis on the quality of the output of production. In other aspects there is commonality between this and Lean. This book will not explore Six Sigma further.

SUMMARY

Making systems more efficient is an effective way of doing proactive problem management.

CHAPTER 13
APPLYING THE PRINCIPLES TO THE WORLD OUTSIDE OF IT

Having looked at the application of problem-solving techniques to the IT world, this chapter reflects on whether those techniques are applicable to a wider audience. We have seen that Lean techniques, which originated within the automotive industry, have been mapped across to the IT world and have proved valuable in understanding the waste within IT systems. It may be argued that in the same way, the problem-solving techniques which have grown up in the IT world are applicable to other fields.

FIXING YOUR HEATING SYSTEM

Many homes in the UK are heated using a central heating system powered by a gas boiler. There are a small number of active components in a central heating system, and it is not that difficult to diagnose faults if one has a basic understanding of how they interoperate. This can obviate expensive plumber callouts or at the very least ensure that the plumber only fixes (and charges for) work that is necessary.

There are six key components to the control of a central heating system:

- the control unit is an electronic device which turns the other components on and off according to input signals and a timer
- the gas boiler heats up the water when the control unit determines that it should – it may have an internal thermostat to protect itself and to limit the maximum temperature of the water

- the pump circulates the water around the system – this is either on or off and often has a light to indicate which state it is in; it may also have three speeds but note, that faster may not be better
- the room thermostat will send a signal to the control unit to turn off the heating of the radiators once the ideal temperature has been reached
- the cylinder thermostat will send a signal to the control unit to turn off the heating of the hot water cylinder once the ideal temperature has been reached
- the gate valve is placed at a T junction in the pipework with the pump upstream from it, the cylinder off one leg of the T and the central heating radiators off the other leg. The gate valve can be in one of three positions, allowing water to flow either just to the cylinder, just to the radiators or to both at the same time. The gate valve is the part which fails most frequently in my personal experience, and it is useful to note that it has a manual bypass feature which allows the system to continue to operate (albeit sub-optimally) should the gate valve fail. The manual bypass places the gate valve in the mid-position, providing heat to both the cylinder and the radiators.

If your heating system suddenly stops working, then *divide and conquer* techniques may be applied to try to identify which of the above components is at fault. Obviously if there is a water leak, then that needs to be attended to and the system re-filled with water before anything else can be done.

If the heating system fails, then the first task is to collect data and a *timeline*. Is the system still producing hot water at all? Is it still producing central heating at all? What temperature are various pipes around the different components? Is the temperature constant or does it vary according to time of day?

It is worth switching the control unit between various options and collecting data for each setting:

- Hot water on; central heating (radiators) off
- Hot water off; central heating on
- Both on
- Both off

If the pipes get hot, then this would suggest that the gas boiler is working and that the pump is working. If the gas boiler comes on but no pipes get hot, just lukewarm, then the pump may have failed. If either heating or hot water is working fine but the other is not working at all, this usually indicates that the gate valve has failed. At this point, using the manual override lever on the gate valve should restore service to both halves (albeit that it may not reach full temperature). If the manual override works, then the gate valve is not working or the power to the gate valve is not working.

If using the manual override makes no difference, then the thermostats should be considered and ruled out.

When we first moved into our current house the heating system was working, but sub-optimally. After having the radiators upgraded to having individual thermostats with no discernible improvement, I determined that one of the active components must be faulty. I had a spare control unit, so I tried replacing that, but it made little difference. I brought in a plumber and took advice. They suggested that the pump probably needed changing and replaced it. It didn't make much difference. I contacted another plumber by email and gave them the symptoms and asked them what they would do next, without telling them that the pump had already been replaced. They said that the pump needed replacing. I contacted the original plumber and asked them to look at the gate valve. They said that they had looked at it during the first visit, and they didn't think the gate valve was faulty but agreed to replace it (since I was paying). It was only when they removed the wet side of the gate valve that we found out that the flap which should form the gate within the pipework had broken in half and was not making a good seal. Although the motor was rotating the paddle, the paddle was making no difference to the system without the flap on the end of it. Replacing the whole gate valve unit fixed the problem.

Two years later, the electromechanical side of the gate valve failed and I was able to diagnose and replace it for myself at considerably less cost than the visit from the plumber.

If one has a toolbox of problem solving techniques, they may be applied in all walks of life.

SUMMARY

Although this book describes problem management and problem solving from an IT perspective, the same techniques may be applied in all walks of life.

CHAPTER 14
USING CHECKLISTS

In his book *The Checklist Manifesto: How to Get Things Right*, Atul Gawande describes how *checklists* are a valuable resource in all walks of life. They are a valuable tool in both proactive and reactive problem management. The obvious example is in the use of the *Drill Down* technique. One can apply the Drill Down technique using personal experience in order to know what question to ask next. There are two reasons why this is sub-optimal. The first, which is a main theme of Gawande's book, is that we all forget items from a list. If my wife gives me a shopping list of items to buy from the store, then if I try to remember the list it is quite likely that I will remember most of the items, but I will sometimes forget one or two items. The same will be true of applying the Drill Down technique just using personal experience – one will forget certain questions or ask them in the wrong order. In comparison, if I write a shopping list for the store which is laid out in the order in which I walk around the store and my wife ticks the items we want this week, then my accuracy is improved. This is the principle for the Drill Down technique – the right questions in the right order.

The second reason is that using personal experience works extremely well for the expert who has been doing the job for many years, but it is very difficult to transfer that knowledge to the new starter. If there is a written down checklist of questions to ask, then that list can be given to the new starter and they will be at near full speed within a very short period of time.

In terms of my shopping list, this proved useful during the Covid-19 pandemic of 2020/21 when I had to self-isolate for a week and could not do my weekly shop. The shop offered an online facility, but on a three-week lead time, which was of no use. A friend offered to do the shopping for me. I was able to send them a printed list with not only the items we required but also the aisles in the store where they would find them.

Checklists are also useful in other stages of *problem management*, to remind people to consider all the options. We typically look at six different possible cause and effects (Chapter 8), and a checklist may be useful to ensure that all have been considered. Checklists are really useful during problem boards to ensure that all items of the agenda have been covered off.

Some sample checklists are provided in Appendix B.

SUMMARY

Building a set of checklists for your own circumstances is a valuable way of ensuring that each problem is dealt with in a consistent way and that steps are not forgotten.

CONCLUSION

> 'Oh, how I wish I could shut up like a telescope! I think I could, if only I knew how to begin.' For, you see, so many out-of-the-way things had happened lately, that Alice had begun to think that very few things indeed were really impossible.
> – Down the Rabbit-Hole, *Alice's Adventures in Wonderland*, Lewis Carroll

Problem management is sometimes ignored as being too difficult, if not impossible. It is true that it is not always possible to find or fix the *root cause* of a *problem*, but that is not a reason not to try. This book has presented a toolbox full of different tools for tackling problems. Different problems will require different tools in the same way that different DIY challenges require different tools. Hopefully, you have not only increased your own toolbox, but also now have a greater understanding of which tool to use when. Telescopes allow us to see stars and planets in far more detail than we could possibly see with the naked eye, and in the same way, problem management techniques allow us to home in on problems and see their behaviour in a way which is just not consistently possible using ad hoc techniques.

Your next challenge is taking these techniques and applying them in your own organisation. If you are not sure where to begin, remember the advice of the King in Alice in Wonderland:

Begin at the beginning and go on till you come to the end: then stop.

APPENDIX A

GLOSSARY

Term	Description	Chapter of First occurrence
5 Whys	A problem solving technique for exploring why a problem has arisen	11
Artificial Intelligence	The ability for automated tools to learn for themselves, providing traits of problem solving	5
Automation	Repeatable actions performed by computers without human interaction	5
BAU	'Business as usual' distinguishes between work conducted as part of a project and the BAU work which is needed to keep a system working, i.e. it is normal operations.	9
Cause	The original action which gives rise to an incident or problem	1
Change Enablement	A formal process for the management of technical changes to IT services and systems	2
Chaotic Problem	A problem with no discernible root cause	4
Checklists	Ordered lists of items/tasks/questions	6 / 14
Communication	The exchange of information between teams	8
Complex Problem	A problem with multiple root causes	4
Complexity Theory	Categorising problems into groups according to how they should be tackled	4
Complicated Problem	A problem with a single root cause which is not initially obvious	3

Term	Description	Chapter of First occurrence
Configuration Items	Computer assets which need to be accounted for and are subject to change enablement (such as desktops, laptops, servers, printers, network switches and the software which runs on them)	10
Continual Improvement	A formal process for deciding what improvements need to be made to a service and prioritising those changes	9
Cynefin Framework	A specific complexity theory	4
Demand	The quantity or capacity of a service required by its customers at a given moment in time	2
Development System	A duplicate version of the system which delivers a service, whereby development work and/or testing may be conducted without risk to the production service	4
DHCP	The Dynamic Host Configuration Protocol (DHCP) is a network management protocol used for automatically assigning IP addresses to computers.	3
Divide and Conquer	A problem-solving technique whereby the problem is broken into parts and each part tackled separately	4 / 7
DNS	The Domain Name System (DNS) resolves IP names (such as web page URLs) into IP addresses.	3
Drill Down	A problem-solving technique for reducing the number of possible causes of an incident or problem	6
Effect	The result of a particular cause	1
Environment	The surroundings or context in which equipment operates (such as whether it is air-conditioned or not)	8
Equipment	The physical components of a system	8
Event	Something that has happened	1

Term	Description	Chapter of First occurrence
Fail over	When a resilient system stops using a component and instead relies on an equivalent, duplicate component. E.g. if a server has dual power supplies and one power supply fails, then the server will 'fail over' to using only the other power supply	1
Failure Mode	A specific way in which a system could fail	3
Impact	How much effect the issue is having on users – the extent to which it is preventing them from doing their job	1
Incident Management	The formal process for managing incidents	10
Incidents	An unplanned interruption to a service or reduction in the quality of that service[1]	0
IP	Internet Protocol is the network communications protocol which undergirds the internet	6
ITIL 4	A framework which sets out formal processes and practices for managing incidents, problems, change enablement, and much more–a best practice way of doing ITSM	1
ITSM	IT Service Management–the formal management of services	
ITSM Tool	An application which allows the Service Desk and other IT teams to manage the records associated with incidents, problems and changes	2
Known Error	A problem which has been analysed but not resolved	10
Lean	A methodology for improving efficiency	12
Method Statement	A detailed list of operations in order to effect a change (a recipe)	2

Appendix A

Term	Description	Chapter of First occurrence
Obvious Problem	A problem with a single root cause which has been observed before and may be discerned without significant investigation	4
Patterns of Business Activity	Routine fluctuations in the demand of a business according to time of day, week, month or year	2
People	The human aspects of the provision of a service	8
Presenting Issue	The symptoms of a problem as perceived by the user, which may not be a true reflection of the root cause	6
Problem	A cause, or potential cause, of one or more incidents[2]	0
Problem Board	Typically a formal meeting established to address a specific problem	11
Problem Management	The formal process for managing problems	0
Process	A documented series of actions	8
RAID Disks	Redundant Array of Inexpensive Disks – an arrangement of data on a set of disks in such a way as to optimise the disks which may be used to facilitate resilience such that the loss of one disk does not result in any loss of data (dependent on the RAID level chosen)	3
Resilience	The ability for a system to continue to provide its main service despite the failure of an individual component	3
Risk	A possible event, which could occur, which may have a positive or negative impact on a service	1
Root Cause	The original cause/event which resulted in the observed behaviour	1
Root Cause Analysis	The analysis of a problem in order to ascertain the original cause/event which resulted in the observed behaviour	1

Term	Description	Chapter of First occurrence
Service	The provision of a product/system and its support to customers in such a way that they derive value from it	1
Service Desk	The first point of contact for users of a service when they need assistance	3
Service Owner	The person accountable for the provision of a service	2
Shift Left	The process of enabling an issue to be tackled at an earlier point by a less qualified individual (e.g. providing service desk analysts with remote access tools which obviate the need for engineers to visit on site)	5
Status Page	A system which provides availability information about services	6
Strategy	The overall plan for achieving goals	8
Stratified Questions	Questions which help to place the user in context rather than specifically to address the presenting issue	6
System	The technology which underpins a service	2
Technical Debt	The direct or indirect cost of addressing (or not addressing) the issues resulting from problems which have been accepted or ignored and for which there are no plans to fix	10
Timeline	The sequence in which events take place	2
Urgency	How quickly the business needs an issue addressed.	10
URLs	The Uniform Resource Locator is the formal term for the address for a web page typically seen at the top of a web browser window	
Workaround	A temporary method of working which avoids the impact of a problem without fixing it.	1

Notes

1 ITIL Foundation: ITIL 4 Edition, Axelos Ltd, Stationery Office, 2019
2 ITIL Foundation: ITIL 4 Edition, Axelos Ltd, Stationery Office, 2019

APPENDIX B
SAMPLE CHECKLISTS

PROBLEM BOARD AGENDA

- Impact–
  - how serious is this problem?
  - what is the impact of it on the business?
  - how many users are affected?
- Urgency – how quickly does it need to be resolved?
- Workarounds – are there any workarounds for the users affected by this problem?
- The timeline of the problem – when did users first start noticing the problem? Is there any system information such as event logs which would indicate when the problem first occurred?
- Changes – the change records in the ITSM tool should be compared with the timeline to identify whether the problem has been caused by a planned change
- Plausible causes of the problem and any techniques which could be used to corroborate or eliminate specific causes should be discussed
- What further diagnostic information is required to investigate this further?
- Do we have the right people available?
- Agreed actions (SMART)

CAUSE AND EFFECT TO CONSIDER

- Strategy
- Environment
- Communication
- People
- Processes
- Equipment

DRILL DOWN TECHNIQUE

Stratified questions (i.e. questions not directly related to the issue, but which help to put the issue in context)

1. Name, location, and department of user
2. Has user experienced this issue before?
3. Is anyone else nearby to the user also experiencing the issue?
4. Has anything changed recently (e.g. have they moved office)?
5. When was the last time they restarted/shutdown and started their computer?
6. Is this a desktop or a laptop?

Direct questions

1. Do we know whether the service is up and running?
2. Is everything else working?
3. When was it last working/when did it stop working?
4. What is the behaviour – is there an error message?

Network

1. Is it just you or are other users affected?
2. Is this wired or are you using Wi-Fi?
3. Does the wired PC have lights illuminated alongside the network socket?
4. What does the diagnostics command reveal? (e.g. run *cmd.exe* and type *ipconfig/all*)

INDEX

Index

Printed in the United States
by Baker & Taylor Publisher Services